YOU'RE BUSY.
I GET IT.

QUICK TIPS TO ACCOMPLISH MORE WITH LESS STRESS

JOAN WASHBURN

You're Busy. I Get It.
© 2018 Joan Washburn. All rights reserved.

No part of this publication may be reproduced, stored in a retrieval system, or transmitted in any form or by any means, electronic, digital, mechanical or photocopying, recording, scanning, or otherwise, except for inclusion in a review or as permitted under Sections 107 and 108 of the United States Copyright Act, without either prior written permission of the Publisher, or authorization through payment of the appropriate per-copy fee to the Copyright Clearance Center.

Published in the United States by Joan Washburn
www. .com

978-1-62967-127-7 (p)
978--------- (e)

Book and cover design by Robin Krauss, www.bookformatters.com

PRAISE FOR *YOU'RE BUSY. I GET IT.*

We are all "busy" with our work life and our personal life. Finding a balance between the two can challenge anyone. One of my personal challenges was taking time to read, understand and apply the advice of "self-help" books. I found *You're Busy. I Get it.* to be practical AND engaging. This short book it is full of sound, constructive advice, which you can relate to and use in your everyday life!

Sue Buckley Halliday,
Healthcare Consultant

Joan Washburn's book, *You're Busy. I Get It.*, is a must read for busy professionals. I love its short chapters with actionable tips so I didn't have to read everything all at once before I could start implementing the ideas. I could relate to the content in her chapters – she truly understands busy professionals and offers ideas that are doable.
Pat Altvater

AFP Marketing,
Author, *Choose Success - Ignite the Power Within*

Professional and personal self-help in small bites! Each delicious chapter is fuel for a successful powerful life! Big punch minimalism! Loved it! Thank you Joan!

Terri Bergman,
Gourmet Business Owner

At every turn of the page I was given a real tool to improve my game and even a Quick Tip on how to put it to use. If that wasn't enough, the way Joan writes is like she is sitting here with me personally. This combination leads to success...with less stress!

Lori Gorrell,
Chief Growth Officer, Upward Solutions Coaching and Consulting

Dedicated to my Dad.

ACKNOWLEDGEMENTS

"Gratitude unlocks the fullness of life."
— Melody Beattie

I would like to thank Dr. Maria Nemeth, Rev. Beth Ann Suggs and Mr. Wayne Manning for teaching and supporting me in living the basic principle: "Look, See, Tell the Truth and take Authentic Action."

My colleagues, life coaches, Kris Thaller, Penny Kowal and Lori Gorrell, for their ever present support, encouragement and masterful coaching.

My wonderful clients. Each of you has contributed more to my life than you will ever know.

My Dad for all his love and guidance.

And my biggest fan in heaven, my Mom. Please ask the Lord to bless my work.

CONTENTS

Introduction		1
1.	To Your Success	3
2.	Are You a "Busyholic"?	7
3.	Bad News for Multi-taskers	9
4.	Spotting Driven Behavior	11
5.	"Squirrel!"	13
6.	The Danger of Perfectionism	17
7.	Never be Late Again	19
8.	A Time Management Tip	21
9.	How to Spark Your Creativity	23
10.	Laughter, Learning and Horses	25
11.	When Smaller is Sweeter	27
12.	How to Stop Losing Your Keys	29
13.	Life's Everyday Obstacles – Gotta Love 'em	31
14.	The Value of Plan B	33
15.	Leadership and Acknowledgement	35
16.	My Favorite Definition of Leadership	37
17.	Taming Your Thoughts	39
18.	The Case for Celebrating	41
19.	The 5 Criteria of a Powerful Vision	43
20.	3 Rules for Delegating with Ease	45

21.	Are you part of the 87%	47
22.	Mix it up!	49
23.	No Groaning Allowed	51
24.	The Power of a Promise	53
25.	The One Sure Way to Look Totally Competent	55
26.	What's Your Excuse?	57
27.	Sleep On It	59
28.	Lighten up	61
29.	Hope-based Decision Making	63
30.	Ask the Expert	65
Resources		67
The Author		69

INTRODUCTION

Sometimes when you don't know what to do, it's best to just follow the path that shows up in front of you, especially if it calls to your heart. That's how I got into coaching. For 27 years I had been in the medical diagnostic imaging industry. I started out as a sales person and 20 years later was VP of Sales and Marketing. I worked hard, was incredibly busy, was very successful and loved it! Well, most of it. I worked with amazing people and our work made a difference in people's lives. Then in 2004 we were bought out by a multi-national conglomerate. Within a few months the consolidation began. Shortly after that I was out of a job.

It was a scary. I had never been out of work in my life. At the same time it was a little exciting. I was at a point in my life where I could do whatever I wanted to do as opposed to automatically taking the next step on the corporate ladder. But what exactly was that? What did I want to do next?

During that time I was in CA reconnecting with a friend I hadn't seen in a while. We were in the parking lot after a yoga class when she ran into someone she knew. He had just completed a four day course at the Academy for Coaching Excellence (ACE) called, Mastering Life's Energies. He was incredibly excited about what he'd learned and the positive impact it had on his life. He felt he had a lot more clarity and was able to focus like never before. His enthusiasm was contagious. After doing some research, I signed up.

I remember one of my first thoughts when the course was only half over – "I wish I had known this stuff long ago". I wouldn't have changed any of the major decisions I'd made in my life, but I would have lived with so much more ease and grace as opposed to the stress and struggle I experienced so much of the time.

Now, as a faculty member of that same Academy for Coaching Excellence, I teach the many principles I learned and I coach busy, stressed out executives, like I used to be. As a coach I support my clients as they accomplish what is important to them, both personally and professionally, with a sense of ease.

This book contains many of the things I learned at ACE as well as a few other things I learned along the way in the school of hard knocks. At the very back is a Notes page where you can document your thoughts and actions. My goal is for you to achieve what is really important to you with as much ease and grace as possible. Each page includes one tip you can put to use THAT DAY as my way to support you here and now. Then when you have a few minutes read another one – in any order you want. Because "You're Busy! I get it!"

CHAPTER 1

TO YOUR SUCCESS

"Success is consistently doing what you said you would do with clarity, focus, ease and grace."
— Maria Nemeth, Ph.D.

Imagine – what would your life be like? What could you accomplish by "consistently doing what you said you would do with clarity, focus, ease and grace"?

This definition changed my mindset on the concept of "Success" when I heard it for the first time studying at the Academy for Coaching Excellence. Moreover, learning to live by this simple statement has been one the biggest contributors to my own personal achievement and happiness. This definition covers everyone, regardless of what your goals are – big or small, personal or professional. It's so simple and yet all-encompassing. Let's take a closer look.

CONSISTENTLY. Think about someone you know well who is very successful. I'll bet they are reliable, very dependable; people can count on them simply because they do what they said they would do. Where do you sit on the "Do what you said you would do" scale?

"Most the time", it is very important to me,

"Some of the time", it's not something I focus on, or

"Rarely" - I really need to work on that.

CLARITY. I like to think of it as our internal GPS. When you are really clear about your destination, the route to get there becomes obvious. People who have clarity know 2 things. First, they know what is important to them; and second, they know the steps they need to take to get them there. Clarity keeps you from overcommitting, becoming overwhelmed; and getting distracted by the "shiny object" syndrome! (More on this "syndrome" in chapter 5.)

FOCUS. Success takes energy and that's where focus comes in. Energy must be directed somewhere. It's imperative you direct your valuable energy and resources precisely where they are needed most so you can accomplish what you desire. Focus is a very powerful thing because what you focus on is what you make happen. So focus on your destination, whether it is a report that is due or a promised outing for the kids. Imagine the joy and satisfaction reaching that goal will bring to you and others.

EASE. The road to success is twisting, turning, obstacles are thrown in our path, and some sections are a really high and difficult to climb. It can wear out the most resilient of us. How do we reach our goals with ease? By keeping it simple . . . .not making it harder than it needs to be. Just take the next step on your path. Working with clarity and focus and without wasting energy or a struggle from over commitment.

GRACE. The definition of grace is refined movement. Imagine succeeding with a sense of simple elegance and kindness, with dignity and honor? You can and here is how: The doorway to grace is gratitude. Practice gratitude for even the smallest results. Don't wait until you reach your goal. Allow yourself to be truly grateful for all the progress you make along the way.

> **QUICK TIP**
>
> Spend some quiet time imagining what could you accomplish by "consistently doing what you said you would do with clarity, focus, ease and grace"?

CHPATER 2

ARE YOU A "BUSYHOLIC"?

"Beware the barrenness of a busy life."
— Socrates

All of the insights and inspirations in the world mean nothing if you don't take authentic action to make the changes you want. What do I mean by "Authentic Action"? It might be better to begin this conversation with what it isn't.

Imagine a swarm of flies buzzing around on a hot summer's day. There's lots of movement and noise but no direction. In my world we call this "busyholism" – busy all the time, but no fulfillment.

Authentic Action is exactly the opposite. It has clear purpose and a laser-like focus on that purpose, so it moves you forward as opposed to running in place, spinning or stuck. It's usually simple and obvious once we are able to notice it. Let's take a look:

It's important to know that there are two distinct types of Authentic Action.

Type 1: This type of action is all about clearing unfinished business.

Examples include:
- Organizing your office closet, garage, or storage shed
- Making amends for a rude remark to a family member, friend or co-worker.

- Getting your annual physical exam

None of these are fun, but doing them releases pent-up energy and resources that you can now put toward your goal.

Type 2: This type of action takes energy and focuses it upon the goal itself. The result is noticeable progress toward making it happen. It's accompanied by a sense of joy at the accomplishment, a feeling of being in tune with your values.

Examples include:
- Writing a tip a day for your book (what I did for this one!)
- Opening a vacation savings account with $200.00
- Sign up for dancing lessons to waltz at your daughter's wedding.

The Authentic Action you take can be small. It is not the bigness of the action that matters, but that it is focused on what matters to you.

QUICK TIP

The next time you find yourself saying "I would love to, but I am so BUSY!", stop and take a few minutes to really look to see if it is just more of the same old "busyholism" or if you are actually busy moving forward on the things that really matter to you.

When you begin to observe when you are taking Authentic Action toward what you really want to achieve or just busy, it will make all the difference in the world!

CHAPTER 3

BAD NEWS FOR MULTI-TASKERS

"To do two things at once is to do neither."
— Publius Syrus

Do you ever clean out your email inbox when listening to a conference call at work?

What about taking a call from a colleague when at your child's baseball game?

"There's just so much to do each day" you say. "I have to do at least two things at once or I'll never get everything done!"

Well, I hear you. But, just like I cannot take a sip of coffee and talk to you at the same time, our brains cannot process two separate events.

Recent neuroscience research* tells us that the brain doesn't really do tasks simultaneously as we once thought. In fact, we just switch tasks quickly. Each time we move from listening in on the conference call to writing an email or talking to someone, there is a stop/start process that goes on in our brains. That start/stop/start process is a real energy waster. Rather than saving time, it costs time (even very small micro seconds). It's less efficient, we make more mistakes, and over time it can be energy zapping.

Not only that, but trying to do too many things at once causes the brain to actually lose the capacity for deep thinking altogether!

The thing is we may be able to rapidly switch between tasks, but we are not able to do so in any depth. The result is that eventually we just end up just skimming across the surface of tasks at hand. In the long-term it actually changes the brain from being able to focus deeply on a single task well, to one that wants to jump around a lot.

If you don't believe me check out the article "The Myth of Multi-tasking" by Dr. Nancy K. Napier. The link to this article is on the Resources page of my website: www.washburnendeavours.com.

QUICK TIP

Next time you think you're multi-tasking, stop and be aware that you are really switch-tasking. Then give yourself a time limit (10 minutes, 45 minutes?) – Whatever the task requires - and focus on just that one task.

See if you can't complete it better, faster, and with less energy.

CHAPTER 4

SPOTTING DRIVEN BEHAVIOR

"Sometimes doing less accomplishes more."
— Joan

Are you used to going full tilt all day, every day and often late into the night?

If something isn't working for you, do you do more of it - just a little bit harder?

Well, as much as it might seem like a good idea at the time, that's not always the best course of action. It is actually "Driven Behavior". You may have heard yourself described as "Driven" and that can be a good thing, but it can also include habits that are holding you back. The key is to know the difference.

Here are the 3 Symptoms of Driven Behavior (the kind you DON'T want):

1) **Repetition:** You think or do something over and over even if it causes needless effort and does not move you forward. Even when you get frustrated, angry or sad about it, you continue the behavior or thought.

2) **Limited Satisfaction:** There is no joy in Driven Behavior. We feel compelled to fill every waking hour with an item on our "to do" or

"should do" lists – much of which gives us limited or short-lived satisfaction.

3) And lastly, (my personal favorite): Perfectionism: "Just one more finishing touch." Nothing is quite good enough to be considered complete. It robs us of the feeling of a job well done. Perfectionists often feel they haven't done anything well enough. It can masquerade as virtue, but be careful – most often it's an excuse for not producing the result you promised.

QUICK TIP

Take some quiet time to look at the 3 symptoms - **Repetition, Lack of Satisfaction** and **Perfectionism** - notice where they apply in your life. Write it down.

Take a deep breath and be compassionate with yourself. Your goal here is to uncover where your own Driven Behavior has kept you from focusing your energy effectively, not to beat yourself up over it.

The clearer this becomes, the more quickly you can begin to take Authentic Actions – those that move you toward things that really matter to you.

Also, don't be surprised to notice that often doing LESS toward what really matters to you will reward you with MORE satisfaction, fulfillment and enjoyment.

CHAPTER 5

"SQUIRREL!"

"Certain things catch your eye, but only follow those that capture the heart."
— Ancient Indian Proverb

Every successful person I have ever known by their very nature, sees opportunities all around them. They notice ways to make things better, meet a need, or fix a problem.

However, this acute awareness can become their greatest weakness if not kept in check. Often it's not a lack of ideas that keeps them from achieving things, but having TOO MANY ideas to choose from! There are just so many shiny things to distract us!

But not all that glitters is gold.

"Shiny Object" Syndrome is the tendency to get distracted by new thoughts and ideas, and never focus on or complete anything. It can lead to a state of constant distraction where we continually lose ourselves in imagination and dreaming, instead of staying focused on accomplishing our goals.

You've experienced it, I'm sure. It looks like this:

- In the middle of a challenging project, you decide to check your email, peruse a favorite newsfeed, Facebook, or Twitter. An hour later you go back to the project and have to reorient yourself as to where you were before you can continue.

- You're always ready to take on a new project, even if your workload is heavy, because the allure of a new challenge is just more than you can resist. There's such great energy and excitement in starting something new!
- You're constantly starting new ideas only to move on to the next one as soon as implementing the first idea gets difficult. For example, you start a new workout program, then drop it for the latest craze, never reaching your original fitness goal.

Basically, you constantly start things, but often don't finish them before you are on to the next shiny object. Sound Familiar?

Don't worry, it's not fatal, but it can cause you to fill up your day with busyness, as opposed to authentic actions that move you toward that important goal. You waste countless hours and dollars in pursuit of a new shiny object when you haven't thought through whether this new item, technique, service or product is "right" for your business or your life.

When we are chasing after shiny objects instead of taking focused action toward what's important to us, we become frustrated, disappointed in ourselves, and downright weary. At the end of the day we begin to question our commitment and even the goal or dream we started out for in the beginning.

> ## QUICK TIP
>
> Here are some very effective steps you can take to avoid being distracted by shiny objects once and for all. I call them the 3 C's.
>
> **First, CHOOSE 1** – do your homework, form a focus group, get professional advice - then Choose 1 idea! Stop procrastinating, making excuses and wasting precious time and energy chasing every shiny object that comes along. Focus!
>
> **Second, COMMIT** to the time, money, energy, resources – whatever it's going to take to accomplish it. When things get tough, as they always do, just take the next small step in front of you. Keep your eyes on the prize! Be committed to see it through to the finish! Stay focused!
>
> **Third,** my personal favorite, **CELEBRATE** your results! – Too often we forget to celebrate before moving on to the next idea. When you celebrate your results it renews your spirit. It gives you the energy to choose the next idea wisely and make it a reality.

Also, Jack Canfied has written an article with some great advice on how to beat the Shiny Object Syndrome posted on the Resources page of my website: www.washburnendeavours.com.

CHAPTER 6

THE DANGER OF PERFECTIONISM

"Good enough is good enough. Perfect will make you a big fat mess every time."
— Rebecca Wells,
The Crowning Glory of Calla Lily Ponder

If you've been called a perfectionist and you're not a brain surgeon, this is for you!

I had been working on a big project for a really long time. It was good, but I didn't want to put it out there until it was perfect. As a result, it was taking a lot longer than it needed to and I wasn't able to achieve the results I wanted. When my friend said it was because I was being a perfectionist, the coach in me perked up! So, I dotted the last "i" crossed a few t's and got it out there. The results were terrific!

I was reminded of the dangers of perfectionism. You might even think of it as a quality or trait, but all it does is stress you out and slow you down.

- It robs you of the joy and satisfaction of completing something; of experiencing a job well-done.
- It keeps your energy all tied up in almost completed projects.
- It's a fast track to frustration and unhappiness.

Over 20 years of research Paul Hewitt, PhD, found that perfectionism correlates with depression, anxiety, eating disorders and other mental health problems.

So, if you have a tendency to make modification after modification saying "just one more finishing touch"; if there is something big you keep putting off doing because you're just not quite ready, or if you have some unfinished projects weighing you down, here's a 3-step QUICK TIP from a coach who knows exactly how you feel –

> **QUICK TIP**
>
> 1. Get an outside perspective! Is it "good enough"?
> 2. Make final edits, if suggested.
> 3. Get your brilliance, your creativity, and your ideas out there!
>
> Because often we're the last to see just how fantastic our work is. It may not be "perfect", but fantastic none the less!

CHAPTER 7

NEVER BE LATE AGAIN

"Leave time for error."
— My Mom

Here is something my very wise Mother taught me that immediately eliminated a great deal of stress from my life.

One day I had 2 appointments out of town and my Mom and I decided to make a day of it. The meetings were an hour apart and so I scheduled the day accordingly. (You can probably see where this is going). The problem began when we ran into some unexpected construction on the way to the first meeting. I began to stress knowing I would be late for that meeting, which would mean I would also be late for the second meeting. Things went from bad to worse when got caught in a traffic jam - making us even later. I was really panicking now as I just HATE being late. My Mom could see my distress and in a quiet calm voice she said "You don't leave any time for error, do you Joan?"

I have to say I was kind of stunned. The thought of "leaving time for error" had never occurred to me. I was one of those people who scheduled every minute to the minute – no time to "waste". I don't do that anymore.

QUICK TIP

Add a minimum of 15 minutes to your expected arrival time for nearly everything you do.

If you get there early you'll have a little time to either get centered for the meeting, a 5 minute phone call or maybe even a quick email check and response (for those of you who also feel the need to fill up every minute!).

So, give it a try and see if it doesn't lower your stress level a little each day.

CHAPTER 8

A TIME-MANAGEMENT TIP

"This is the key to time management - to see the value of every moment."

— Menachem Mendel Schneerson

As a Coach the two main reasons people give me for not doing that thing they've been wanting to do for a long time are: "I don't have the time" or "I don't have the money".

Regarding Money – it touches everything and I can't cover it in a page. However, I can recommend a wonderful book, *The Energy of Money*, by Dr. Maria Nemeth. It will transform the way you look at money as well as a lot of other valuable things.

Today I want to focus on the one thing we all have the exact same amount of – TIME. All of us have 1,440 minutes of time each day.

Someone once said that God invented time to keep everything from happening at once.

In fact, humans invented time to help bring order, meaning and understanding to their unique existence. But often we lose that order, meaning and understanding in a flurry of constant activity.

We wear ourselves out running from the moment we get up until we fall into bed exhausted. Our time is spent working and taking care of others. Or, if we have an extra 10 minutes, we waste it on mindless activities like checking newsfeeds and social media.

Now, I understand the need to unwind and relax. I too have my favorite TV shows. However, let me ask you a question – What would you do- that you are not doing now- if you had all the time in the world? What would you do different?

Spend more time with a loved one? Play an instrument? Learn a language? Write a book? Play with your dog!

Maybe it's something you used to really love doing, but now you just don't have the time?

Let's look -

Spending just ten minutes a day for one year toward something you would truly love to accomplish equals 60 hours—the equivalent of a college course. Imagine consistently spending 70 minutes a week / 60 hours a year, on something meaningful to you.

Please don't misunderstand me – I am not recommending you jam every 10 minute interval with something "productive". This can easily lead to that frenzy of activity I mentioned in Chapter 4.

> **QUICK TIP**
>
> Think of that thing you've always wanted to accomplish, but haven't had (or never found) the time to pursue. Now, schedule a minimum of 10 minutes in your day to put toward this fun, meaningful thing.

Imagine – a little over an hour a week, just for you.

CHAPTER 9

HOW TO SPARK YOUR CREATIVITY

"Make an empty space in the corner of your mind. Creativity will instantly fill it."

— Dee Hock

I have found that when it comes to creativity, the problem is never how to get new thoughts into our minds, but how to get the old used up ones that no longer serve us out!

Here's a parable that illustrates what I mean.

A man is trapped on one side of a river, facing great danger and uncertainty. The land on the other side of the river is safe and calm, but there is no bridge to cross to get there, nor any boat or ferry. Intent on crossing, the man is very creative. He builds a raft of logs, sticks and other materials. He lies on the raft and paddles over to the other side. There, he is safe. That raft served him well; but now what should he do with it? Should he carry it around with him as he walks around on land for the rest of his life? Or should he discard it by the side of the river, and go about his ways?

We all carry around a few thoughts, beliefs, opinions, even situations that worked well at some point in our lives, but no longer serve us. Just recently I gave up my paper calendar for the on-line one that it connected to my scheduler. It has made things so much easier and I no longer double book!

> **QUICK TIP**
>
> Take a few quiet moments to look at something that's not working for you anymore. Set it aside.
>
> It's time to make room for something new and exciting to come in.

CHAPTER 10

LAUGHTER, LEARNING AND HORSES

"I am thankful for laughter, except when milk comes out of my nose."

— Woody Allen

I was recently reminded how very important laughter is when learning something new or under a lot of stress. It really can be the best medicine!

One of my favorite things to do now is ride my horse on wooded trails with my friends. But, when I bought my first horse, and started riding as an adult I found out I had a LOT to learn. His name is Charger and I was so excited!

My first experience with a riding instructor left me in tears thinking I had made a huge mistake. I began to think that I should just sell Charger and forget about the dream I'd had since I was a little girl.

Determined to keep him, I signed up for lessons with a different instructor. Given my previous experience, I was really nervous, but willing to try again. As it turns out, this instructor was different . . . special.

What made her different? Why did I absorb more from her than the previous instructor? Because she was funnier than all get out! She told hysterical stories about her first riding experiences that helped me relax. She made me laugh at myself and Charger like I never had before. The moment I began laughing at myself I gained the observational distance needed to learn.

> **QUICK TIP**
>
> Don't hesitate to laugh at yourself. Even a little chuckle can help.
>
> Sometimes we over-achievers take things way too seriously. A little laughter can go a long way.

CHAPTER 11

WHEN SMALLER IS SWEETER

"Chew off a little every day, because it's hard to swallow a whole pie at once."
— Richelle E. Goodrich, *Slaying Dragons*

So, you have this big goal in mind. There are two VERY different ways to proceed. The first is the one that I did for many years – develop an aggressive action plan, then work 60 -80 hours a week to make it happen. There are a couple of possible results from this strategy – 1.) You will burnout and give up or 2.) You reach it and are too exhausted to enjoy your accomplishment.

There is a better way: especially at the very beginning, the Lift-off phase: SMALLER is better. I can't stress it enough – a strategy of small steady steps is the key to accomplishing big goals with ease. Many of us want to race headlong into lift-off. It is at the beginning of a new project that we are the most excited, prone to promise big results and often end up stalled, unable to move.

One reason is that it takes a lot of energy to begin something new. Like a rocket ship that uses 90% of its fuel just getting off the ground – that's the way things go with a new project or goal. Taking small steady steps has been proven to be much more effective than attempting huge gains when first getting started. Plus, this strategy bypasses that stress inducing part of our brain, the amygdala, which gets activated at the very thought of anything big, new and different.

When I first began studying to be a coach, of the many things we were taught, the importance of taking small steady steps at the beginning of a new project is the one that stood out the most for me. I had often made things a lot harder than they needed to be by promising big gains at the beginning. I was one of those talented, successful and exhausted executives who I love to work with now.

> **QUICK TIP**
>
> Look at the action plan you designed for that big goal that lights you up. Does it consist of small steady steps so you can deliver the results you have promised without killing yourself and driving everyone around you crazy? A plan you can implement with ease as opposed to a lot of struggle?
>
> If so, great! If not, take some time to redesign it based on this valuable principle.

CHAPTER 12

HOW TO STOP LOSING YOUR KEYS

> *"The next message you need is always right where you are."*
>
> — Ram Dass

One recent morning I could not find my keys – again. I had an excuse for this forgetfulness – I was moving. I was only moving 7 miles away, but it might as well be 7000!

If you are like me, you find yourself thinking about the next thing on your never-ending to-do list as opposed to what you are doing that very moment. So you move the car and put the keys in a place that wasn't there in the old house – like the candy dish – while you are thinking about the boxes in the master bedroom and where all those clothes will go. So of course, when you go to leave you can't find your keys,

We are all busy, but there are times life just seems to ramp up. Those are the times it can be especially difficult to just be present to the moment you are in. When it is the most challenging, it is the most important.

QUICK TIP

When you have a lot going on (and truthfully, when don't you?), live in and truly enjoy the very moment you are in.

That way you can keep track of your keys and all your other stuff.

CHAPTER 13

LIFE'S EVERYDAY OBSTACLES – GOTTA LOVE 'EM

"A hero is an ordinary individual who finds the strength to persevere and endure in spite of overwhelming obstacles."
— Christopher Reeve

Imagine– you're on a basketball team, and before a game your coach announces the other team couldn't make it, but you're going to play anyway. The game begins, you have the ball, run down the court and make a basket – easy when there's no one blocking your shot. This happens over and over again. How long before you are bored to death? No one wants to lose, but we do want a challenge.

Winning and scoring are great, but if we dig a little deeper we realize that the thrill is in developing our skills so that we can win despite the obstacles.

Obstacles are at the heart of every interesting and worthwhile game. Yes, obstacles – those objections and disruptions intent on blocking our progress. We try to be prepared, but sometimes they just pop up out of nowhere.

They're expected when it comes to sports, but in the game of life the single most noted reason we don't begin to play for what we truly want is fear of the obstacles we know, or even just suspect, we'll encounter. Or – we give up when we run into an unexpected one. Can you imagine being a basketball player, getting blocked by an opponent, and then stopping on the spot and walking off the court because there wasn't supposed to be any opposition? No! Obstacles are an integral part of the game. It's the same with life.

Obstacles are often deflating frustrating events. They can cause us to question ourselves, our abilities and even the goal itself. But what if we saw that what happens when we're challenged is exactly what is supposed to happen? What if we saw obstacles as a sign that we're doing something right, not something wrong? With this understanding, wouldn't we be encouraged to keep going: to develop the needed skill to master the obstacles?

Think back to a peak experience in your life. Weren't you required to learn something new or otherwise stretch yourself beyond your comfort zone?

QUICK TIP

Stop thinking of these events as obstacles, and start thinking of them as invaluable opportunities to grow.

No obstacles = no growth. Remember that they are at the heart of every interesting and worthwhile game and keep just playing to win!

CHAPTER 14

THE VALUE OF PLAN B

> *"Everyone has a plan until they get punched in the mouth."*
> — Mike Tyson

I love to plan. Seems like I am always planning something. I carefully choreograph each step so that everything works out to be happily ever after. The value of planning is pretty self-evident. But more often than not, I find myself dealing with the upside-down, inside-out version where nothing goes as it should. It's at this point that the real test of my resolve comes in.

This is when I ask myself: What am I most interested in?

- The ISSUE or the IDEA?
- The DRAMA or the DREAM?
- My REASONS for not doing what I said I would do or my RESULTS?

The choice is mine. Whichever one I choose is where my energy will be focused. Obviously I choose the second option!

Then, I make any necessary changes to my original "carefully choreographed" plan. This is when resilience and flexibility become more important than adherence to the original plan.

> **QUICK TIP**
>
> Life is not always about perfectly implementing Plan A, but about how you handle Plan B and C and D and so on!
>
> So, take a deep breath and shift gears. You'll get there.

CHAPTER 15

LEADERSHIP AND ACKNOWLEDGEMENT

> *"You get what you reward."*
> — Bob Nelson

The Art of Acknowledgement is key in leading people. When we acknowledge a person we are calling forth what is true about that person. For example – "Excellent presentation this morning Steve. It's obvious this project is very important to you" or "I see where you worked late last night to finish the proposal Maria. Your commitment and enthusiasm are greatly appreciated." Notice it's not just about what they did, but what you see to be true about them or why they did it– they value their work, they are committed, enthusiastic.

An acknowledgement is not just a compliment. A compliment is something you admire about a person and they are easy for people to shrug off – "Nice tie Sam" – "Oh, it's an old one"; or "Good job Brian" – "It was nothing".

One of the key things about acknowledgement is that, because it includes a quality or trait the person knows to be true about themselves, it sets the stage for trust. The person you acknowledge relaxes and is then more apt to accept your guidance.

A Globoforce research study in 2013 showed that 89 percent of people are more motivated by being told what they are doing right than by being told what they are doing wrong, and nearly 80 percent looked for this recognition to be given close to the time of the activity. Like any leadership skill, you must use it often to become proficient.

> **QUICK TIP**
>
> Look for an opportunity to acknowledge at least one person each and every day.

Notice not just the action, but what you see to be true about that person – they are courageous, empowering, supportive, flexible, focused, creative, etc. Then, observe the response you get from the person. Ultimately it will result in your excelling at the most valuable leadership skill of all – bringing out the greatness in others.

CHAPTER 16

MY FAVORITE DEFINITION OF LEADERSHIP

"... All else is trivial."
— Dee Hock

Recently I came across a definition of Leadership that I loved so much that I had to share it with you.

Although published 10 years ago in Fast Company magazine, this quote was new to me. It was written by Dee Hock, the visionary founder and CEO Emeritus of Visa International. Regarding leadership he stated:

"Here is the very heart and soul of the matter of leadership: If you seek to lead, invest 50% of your time leading yourself--your own purpose, ethics, principles, motivation, and conduct. Invest at least 20% leading those with authority over you and 15% leading your peers. Use the remainder to induce those you "work for" to understand and practice the theory. I use the term "work for" advisedly", he states "for if you don't understand that you should be working for your mislabeled "subordinates," you haven't understood anything. Lead yourself, lead your superiors, lead your peers, and free your people to do the same. All else is trivial."

Gives you a lot to think about doesn't it? It covers every relationship a person in a leadership position must master to ensure their success and the success of all those around them.

> **QUICK TIP**
>
> Look to see – where do you spend the biggest percentage of your time? Do you need to make some adjustments?

CHAPTER 17

TAMING YOUR THOUGHTS

"I need a break from my own thoughts."
— Everyone

Do you ever get tired of your thoughts? I know I sure do!

That's because your brain generates anywhere from 12,000 to 60,000 thoughts per day!

98% of those thoughts are the same thoughts you had yesterday and . . . 80% of those thoughts are negative thoughts.

Now wonder you're so exhausted!

What really exhausts us are the thoughts we have that we believe to be true about us or a situation when they're not!

For example have you ever had the thought that you are a failure at your job? A lousy parent? That you just don't have what it takes to make that dream a reality?

The reason we feel guilty, incompetent and worry is because in some small part of our mind we start to think these things to be true when they are not. At that moment it can sound like the truth, but really is it? Is it really true that you're a failure at your job, a bad parent? NO!

These are just thoughts that are not worth listening to. They are the kind of thoughts that put us in the road to failure.

So what's generating these kinds of thoughts?

Rick Hanson, PhD, author of *Hardwiring Happiness*, states that our brain is hardwired with a built in negativity bias. And he gives some examples that point to this bias.

- Suppose you got twenty things done today and made one mistake. What's likely to stick with you as you're falling asleep? Probably the mistake, even though it was just a small part of your day.
- Here's another example - Let's say your boss gives you an excellent performance review that contains just one piece of critical feedback in a bucket of praise, what are you'll likely focus on? That one negative comment.

How do you quiet the voices in your head that have you stuck and spinning as opposed to taking action toward that goal or dream? Here's how: Shift your thoughts to something for which you are grateful right that very minute. It is a proven fact that our brains cannot entertain two different thoughts at the same time. You cannot think about something that worries you and something for which you are grateful at the same time. It's impossible.

QUICK TIP

When worrying about something, and it's getting you nowhere, put those thoughts aside and focus on something for which you are grateful right now. Spend a few moments deep in that heartwarming thought. If the negative thought creeps back in, gently set it aside and go back to gratitude.

CHAPTER 19

THE CASE FOR CELEBRATING

"Celebrate the small results along the way."
— Maria Nemeth, Ph.D.

Most of us wait until the job is complete before we celebrate. We never think to celebrate small victories. We think we don't deserve it because we haven't achieved that milestone yet.

Or – worse yet often we never celebrate at all! We finish one thing and just move right on to the next without even taking a few minutes to say "Wow! Good job! That wasn't easy, but I did it!" This is one of the major causes of burnout. However, when we take some time to celebrate small victories along the way, it gives us the energy to keep going.

If you are in a leadership position it is especially important for you to set the example of celebrating the small victories of your employees or members of your management team. It has been proven that this is one of the best ways to achieve employee satisfaction and increase productivity.

It's easy to celebrate the big wins and milestones, but celebrating the small victories along the way gives us the energy and motivation to keep going when things get tough. Celebrations keep us from giving up when we come up against an obstacle we did not expect.

QUICK TIP

Celebrate your results along the way: At the end of each day, before you leave the office, write down 3 things you accomplished that day. Notice a small victory or positive result that otherwise you would have missed.

This will ensure you end your day with a sense of satisfaction and fulfillment and you will look forward to tomorrow!

CHAPTER 20

THE 5 CRITERIA OF A POWERFUL VISION

"Vision without action is a daydream. Action without vison is a nightmare."
— Japanese Proverb

What is a vision? Your Vision contains your dreams for your life. It's a mental picture of your ideal life. It acts as the foundation for everything that is yet to come.

When you become really clear about the life you would LOVE to live, write it down and start living from it, you will be amazed at the opportunities and resources that emerge to make it happen.

Here are the 5 criteria of a personal vision that will nearly propel you into the life you would love:

1. A Vision is written in the PRESENT tense - "I AM . . . floating down the Mississippi River with friends; sitting in my new sun porch having coffee; riding my horse, my Harley Davidson or driving my new red sports car on a beautiful summer day . . ."

2. Include everything you would like to do, be and have! This is no time to be timid – think big and bold! If it is not a little uncomfortable, it is too small!

3. There is no "HOW" when writing your Vision. Do not worry about the HOW. Only "WHAT" you would love to do, be and have.

4. A Vision is not a strategic plan! As a matter of fact, if you write a plan before writing a Vision, you will put limits and boundaries on your Vision.
5. It must light you up as you read it! You must love it! On a scale of 1 to 10 it must score a ten!

> ### QUICK TIP
>
> Now, curl up in your favorite chair and, keeping these 5 criteria in mind, begin to write the vision for the life you would love to live.
>
> I know it's not easy to find the time to break away from your everyday duties and responsibilities to just dream. But make the time. I promise you it will be worth it!

CHAPTER 22

ARE YOU ONE OF THE 87%?

"Do not compare yourself. Find out what God has placed in your ability."
— Emmitt Smith

Did you know that approximately 87% of the people in the world feel inferior in some way?

The major reasons given for these feelings of inferiority is that we spend way too much time comparing how we're doing with our judgement of how someone else is doing. In other words, comparing our insides to someone else's outsides and not measuring up. We're comparing our behind-the-scenes reel with everyone else's highlight reel.

Comparing ourselves to others and not measuring up is often the reason that we do not take the steps necessary to make that brilliant idea we've had for a very long time a reality. We quit when we compare ourselves to a successful co-worker, a leader in our field, a sports hero or physically fit model on the cover of a fashion magazine. "I'll never be as good as so and so, so why bother trying."

Often subconscious, these feelings of inferiority cause us to freeze up and do nothing or overcompensate by working ourselves into the ground. While comparing ourselves to others may be a natural knee-jerk reaction, it is not the least bit productive.

What we sometimes forget is that we do not have to measure up to any other person in this world. We are neither inferior nor superior to anyone else. God created each of us to be unique and original.

> ## QUICK TIP
>
> Notice when you are feeling inferior. Look to see if you are comparing yourself to someone else and not measuring up. Then shift your thoughts to something much more productive— What do I need to do to be the best possible version of myself? Then do it!
>
> Do this not just for your own self, but for the benefit and contribution only YOU can make to others.

CHAPTER 23

MIX IT UP!

"Leaving my comfort zone became the key to my success."

— Sujan Patel

In a recent study[1] researchers tested the memory of participants by showing them images which were rated as novel, familiar, and very familiar. The best results came when people were shown a novel image, followed by a familiar one. So, while repetition helps with memory, mixing in new information is important too.

The study also showed where putting yourself in new and unfamiliar situations triggers a unique part of the brain that releases dopamine, nature's make-you-happy chemical. Here's the mind-blower; that unique region of the brain is only activated when you see or experience completely new things.

So, while routines make you feel at ease and in control, what a constant routine really does is dull your sensitivities. Think about the times in your life when you've driven the same route repeatedly: after a certain number of trips, you start tuning out most of it. Have you ever had a trip to the office where you barely remember what happened after you got in the car? If you don't get out of your comfort zone once in a while, you might find yourself tuning out much of your life in the same way.

When you go out of your way to experience new things, or when you let new things happen to you, your brain creates brand new neural pathways that fuel your creative spark and enhance your memory.

> **QUICK TIP**
>
> Mix it up! Because there is value in both – the routine and the novel.
>
> It's a new day! Promise yourself that you'll slip a few new and different activities into your everyday routine.

CHAPTER 24

NO GROANING ALLOWED!

"Goals: Life doesn't get any better than this!"
— Maria Nemeth, PhD

If just the thought of creating annual, quarterly or monthly goals makes you groan and want to turn the page, DON'T DO IT– this page is for you!

We've all created goals throughout our lives. Some we have completed; some we lost interest in half way through, and others we totally abandoned. The main reason our goals fall by the wayside is because what we consider to be a goal is actually just another boring task. There is a big difference between a Goal and a Task.

Your Goals show the world what has a great deal of meaning to you and bring a sense of joy. They reflect how you want to be known in this world. They are promises you make to yourself that you fully intend to keep. A goal is a "yes" to something, not a "no". An example of a goal would be "I am biking through the south of France with my friend, Jane, July, 2018." You might need to start a savings account or lose some weight (tasks) to make it happen, but the bike trip is an example of a goal!

Tasks are unfinished items that bring you a sense of relief when they are done. Examples include: getting rid of credit card debt, going for your annual check-up, or finishing your taxes.

It's important you create goals that light up your life and propel you forward; that bring you great joy and renewed energy; goals so exciting that the thought of achieving them sustains you when the inevitable obstacles and challenges pop-up.

> **QUICK TIP**
>
> ... on discerning goals from tasks: When setting Goals ask yourself this question: "When I accomplish this will I experience 'Whew, what a relief. I finally got that done.'" If so, it's a task. However, if you feel "WOW! Life just doesn't get any better than this!" It's a Goal. Go for it!

CHAPTER 25

THE POWER OF A PROMISE

"A promise made is a debt unpaid."
— Robert W. Service

A promise is your word that you will take action on something. It says: "I guarantee this will be done."

Promises need not be big. However, no matter their size, they are powerful. Keeping them moves you forward and ever closer to your goals. Let's look at what happens when you make a promise, keep it, and what happens when we don't keep a promise.

When we make a promise we are compelled to make good on it – to do what we said we would do – it's as simple as that. Making a promise produces an opening that we are pulled forward to close. Here's what I mean by that.

When you don't do what you said you would do, you're left with the tension of incompletion. An unfulfilled promise is a real energy drain. You expend more energy worrying about it than resolving it. You become physically, emotionally, and spiritually tired. So, ultimately it makes it more difficult to move ahead.

It doesn't matter with whom you made your promise or how big or small: not keeping your word is what creates the energy drain. Unfinished business just weighs you down.

When you put your word out there, you create a gap that can only be closed when you do what you said you would do.

An example would be: I recently told a friend I would bring something special to a party she was having. This created a gap, the expectation of something yet to be done. Well, in the hustle of the day, I forgot to bring it. When she asked me about it, I remembered my promise and felt awful. Being the gracious person she is, she brushed it off as no problem, but I still felt awful. There was a gap, a broken promise, a misplaced trust. Luckily, I live close by so I ran home and got it. The gap was filled and the energy field was balanced. All was well.

> **QUICK TIP**
>
> Look for a promise that you just haven't found the time to keep. It's been bugging you, I know. Find the time and resources to make good on that promise.
>
> Large or small – it's still your word.

CHAPTER 26

THE ONE SURE WAY TO LOOK TOTALLY COMPETENT!

"Competence, like truth, beauty, and contact lenses, is in the eye of the beholder."
— Laurence J. Peter

In life we need support to move forward when our doubts, worries and fear are stopping our progress towards our goals. This requires that we locate people from whom we are willing to seek encouragement. When we do so we are generously allowing this person to make a significant contribution in our life. By working together, we both benefit. This mutual support amplifies our own natural courage, faith, confidence and . . . competence.

Even if you know you can do it yourself, that's not always the point. Often it's about making a connection with a fellow human being. When we ask another person for support we are acknowledging their expertise and ability. We are allowing them to contribute significantly to our success.

And yet, we often insist on "doing it alone" - not getting the help or support that we need. Most of us hold on to the myth that if we accept "help" we diminish our achievements, don't deserve praise for our accomplishments, or need a crutch. Have you ever heard yourself say "Everyone's too busy to help me" or "If you want a job done right, do it yourself'"?

A report from Harvard and the Wharton Business School found that, though many people are afraid to ask for support and risk looking incompetent, they've actually got it backwards! People who seek support were thought of as being MORE COMPETENT. Researchers at both Harvard and Wharton can't be wrong!

> ### QUICK TIP
>
> Although you know how to GIVE support, ask yourself – "do I actively seek it?"
>
> Keep in mind successful people are masterful at giving and receiving support.

CHAPTER 27

WHAT'S YOUR EXCUSE?

"He that is good for making excuses is seldom good for anything else."
— Benjamin Franklin

Recently I went to hear the motivational speaker, author, and business consultant, Mathew Kelly. His talk was titled "Living Every Day with Passion and Purpose." Mathew Kelly has dedicated his life to helping people and organizations become the-best-version-of-themselves.

At one point he pointed out something we all need for watch out for when we realize that we need to develop some new habits or discard some old ones to be the best version of ourselves - EXCUSES!

We all have the desire to be happy, to live a life of meaning, but don't we just come up with the best excuses for not doing what it takes?

There are practically as many excuses as there are people on the planet! However, today I am going to zero in on just one, because I hear it a lot!

Some people spend half their lives using the excuse that they are too young and the other half - they are too old!

If that sounds like something you say, here are some fun facts to consider:

If you think you're too young:

- Anne Frank wrote The Diary of Anne Frank when she was 13
- Mozart wrote his first music composition at age 5

- Bill Gates started Microsoft when he was 19 and
- Joan of Arc led the French army to victory at the age of 16

If you think you are too old:
- Beethoven wrote the Ninth Symphony when he was 54 and nearly deaf
- Fauja Singh ran his first Marathon at the age of 84 and his most recent in 2016 at the age of 104!
- Hulda Crooks scaled Mt. Whitney at 101.
- Mother Teresa began her mission to care for the lepers in Calcutta when she was 40.

QUICK TIP

Think about something you really want to accomplish. If you're not making any progress, what's your excuse? Once you see your favorite go-to excuse, just put it aside and take a small step toward that something that really matters to you.

Now is the time!

CHAPTER 28

SLEEP ON IT

"Sleep is the best meditation."
— Dalai Lama

Have you ever woken up with the answer to a problem that nagged you the night before? It's like your brain worked on it while you were sleeping. Guess what – it did!

Many people – especially ambitious, successful people - subscribe to the false belief that if they sleep less they will achieve more. Yet there is a growing body of research proving that a good night's sleep is essential to a productive day.

While sleep is often associated with giving rest to the body, recent research shows that sleep is really more about the brain. While we sleep our brains are hard at work encoding and restructuring information. Therefore, when we wake up our brains may have made new neural connections, thereby opening up a broader range of solutions to a problem, literally overnight!

In a fascinating TED Talk, Jeff Iliff tells us how, while we are asleep - and only then - the brain, in a process totally different from the rest of the body, actually clears away all the toxins that have accumulated in it during the day while it was hard at work. The link to this incredible TED Talk is in the Resources page of my website, www.washburnendeavours.com..

In a Harvard Business Review article, called "Sleep Deficit: The

Performance Killer", Professor Charles Czeisler explains how sleep-deprivation undermines high performance. Professor Czeisler states that pulling an all-nighter or having a week of just 4-5 hours of sleep a night "induces an impairment equivalent to a blood alcohol level of .1%". Think about that! We would never say "This person is a great worker! He's drunk all the time!"

Some good news for the early birds and night owls among us: science shows that even a nap can increase creativity. Recently, I had a late night and very early morning. Later that day I had to drive for about 3 hours to a meeting. I got so tired I had a hard time focusing so I pulled into a Rest Area and within minutes was sound asleep – actually dreaming! 20 minutes later I woke up feeling alert and rested. I was able to contribute to the meeting in a way I never would have been able to without that cat nap.

In a nutshell, sleep allows us to operate at our highest level of contribution so we can actually achieve more in less time.

QUICK TIP

Systematically and deliberately build sleep into your schedule so you can do more, achieve more and explore more each and every day. A friend of mine added a chime notification on her phone when it is time to go to bed.

CHAPTER 29

LIGHTEN UP!

"Lighten up, just enjoy life, smile more, laugh more, and don't get so worked up about things."
— Kenneth Branagh

In my coaching practice I work with real go-getters who take on so much they sometimes feel overwhelmed and pulled off track. What they want is to stay focused so their hard work pays off with their health and relationships intact!

And there's something I've noticed in their coaching sessions lately that might seem familiar to you.

You guys are really hard on yourselves!

I mean – I get it – you have goals, dreams and the desire to make a difference. You have all these wonderful intentions for your life - You want to be financially successful, a well-respected professional, a loving family member and a good and reliable friend - just to name a few! On top of that, many of you are contributing to your community by being involved in a charity or fundraiser for a cause that is important to you.

It's a lot! It is not easy juggling the diverse things on your plate each and every day. And, if you're like my clients, your list is often longer at the end of the day than the beginning!

Then, if you fall short in just one area or one small thing – inevitably THAT'S the thing you'll be thinking about and beating yourself up over at the end of the day. Right? Sound familiar?

Well, it's time to knock it off! It just doesn't serve anyone, especially yourself. All it does is induce more stress, frustration and zaps your precious energy – the LAST thing you need!

> ### QUICK TIP
>
> To break the vicious cycle of self-criticism: At the very end of each and every day write down 3 things you got done that day. Big things, small things – they all matter. If a thought creeps in about something you really wanted to get done that you didn't get to, no problem, just prioritize it for the next day, and go back to thinking about what you DID get done.
>
> Then just kick-back and enjoy the feeling of accomplishment.

CHAPTER 30

HOPE-BASED DECISION MAKING

"Courage is being scared to death and saddling up anyway."
— John Wayne

The number one reason my clients give me for not taking even the smallest step toward a dream they've had for a long time is . . . fear. I'm not referring to fearing a life-or-death situation, I'm referring to the fear that causes us to hang back for no good reason.

Fear–based decision making is when you let your fears or worries dictate your actions (or, in most cases, your lack of action). For example . . .

- "I'd love to take a trip to Israel, but what if something bad happens while I'm there? I'll go somewhere else instead."
- "I'd love to write a book, but what if people hate it? Maybe I'll take one more course on effective writing before starting."

If you can relate, don't worry – you are not alone. Far from it. Research shows that 80 percent of our choices are fear-based; in other words, we're afraid of what will happen if we don't make a certain choice as opposed to making decisions based on what we really want out of life. The unfortunate result is that we don't do the things that we say are important to us.

Here are 5 things to keep in mind when making decisions:

1. Don't pick goals where the stakes are low.
Step out of your comfort zone – get comfortable with feeling uncomfortable!

2. Nobody is rooting for you to fail.
Maybe you'll succeed. Maybe you'll fail. For the most part, nobody cares one way or the other.

3. Just because you don't like where you have to start from doesn't mean you shouldn't get started.
For example: "I'd love to get in shape, but what if I look stupid at the gym? I need to lose some weight before I sign up.

4. Stop making uncertain things, certain.
Keep in mind - Failure is not certain

5. The only real failure is not taking any action in the first place.

One year from today, your life is going to be different; it won't be the same. Whether you've made progress or fallen back is going to be a function of the choices you make between now and then.

QUICK TIP

My wish for you was best said by Nelson Mandela: "May your choices reflect your hopes, not your fears."

CHAPTER 31

ASK THE EXPERT

"An expert knows all the answers - if you ask the right questions."
— Levi Strauss

Do you have a goal that you are very motivated to accomplish, but try as you might, you just can't seem to make any headway? Often our #1 goal is the most elusive!

Luckily, there are Mentors, Sponsors, Consultants, Counselors, "Soft Skills" Trainers, and Life Coaches to help you. But, how do you know which is the best specialty for you to hire to help you reach that specific goal? To make it easy for you I boiled down the expertise of each.

A **MENTOR** is a subject matter expert with experience in the area being mentored. They are sometimes partners, but most often a mentor takes the mentee "under their wing". They often introduce the mentee to other influential people.

A **SPONSOR** is someone who can not only advise you on your career, but actively help advance it. They have power in an organization and can use their social capital and credibility to advocate for you. According to a 2011 Harvard Business Review special report sponsors not only advise their charges, they promote, protect, prepare, and push them.

The **CONSULTANT** is hired by the client to complete a specific job. They give advice, answers and opinions. They are relied on to understand a given problem and provide a solution. The consultant is a partner with the client, however, they may not be invested in the client's personal success.

A **COUNSELOR** helps their client develop insight and/or emotional healing from traumatic events. Until resolved it will be difficult for people to make significant changes in their lives.

The "Soft Skills" **TRAINER** is often the most needed and yet misunderstood. It's often said that hard skills will get you an interview, but you need soft skills to get — and keep — the job! Adaptability, optimism, common sense, a sense of humor, empathy and the ability to collaborate and negotiate are all important soft skills. Other soft skills include situational awareness and the ability to read a situation as it unfolds to decide upon a response that yields the best result for all involved. Successful "Soft Skills" training results in employees who are able to create successful relationships with their colleagues and customers, communicate effectively, and be a contribution to their team.

A **LIFE COACH** works with the client to produce concrete, measureable results. They are seen as a partner. Their clients are in a good place mentally and emotionally, and ready to receive guidance and instruction on how to make changes that will help them achieve their goals.

> **QUICK TIP**
>
> Decide on the type of expertise you need right now then find the very best fit for YOU.

RESOURCES

Maria Nemeth, PhD, *Mastering Life's Energies*, (New World Library, 2007)

Maria Nemeth, PhD, *The Energy of Money and Mastering Life's Energies*, (Random House, 1999)

Rick Hanson, PhD, *Hardwiring Happiness* (Crown Publishing Group, 2017)

https://www.psychologytoday.com/blog/brain-wise/201209/the-true-cost-multi-tasking

https://thinkgrowth.org/leaving-my-comfort-zone-became-the-key-to-my-success-a479e8915452

[1]https://www.mindbodygreen.com/0-23924/the-brain-chemicals-that-make-you-happy-and-how-to-trigger-them.html

www.ted.com/talks/jeff_iliff_one_more_reason_to_get_a_good_night_s_sleep.

The Coaching Guide, Coach Training Program, Academy for Coaching Excellence

JOAN WASHBURN

Executive Coach, Trainer and Speaker

Joan supports her clients to see things in a whole new way that empowers them to move forward toward the things that are really important to them.

She is credentialed by the International Coach Federation, a Faculty Member of the Academy for Coaching Excellence and a graduate of the Wharton Business School's Advanced Management Program.

Her professional development trainings, both live and on-line, are filled with innovative coaching tools and skills proven essential to accelerate career advancement and organizational development.

Coaching is a second career for Joan. In her speaking engagements she always engages the audience with personal stories about what she learned in her 25 years of successful sales, marketing and executive management experience.

To learn more about her work and her Learning Center on her horse farm, Blueberry Hill, contact Joan via her website: www.washburnendeavours.com.

NOTES

NOTES

YOU'RE BUSY. I GET IT.

NOTES